# 60

# S U P E R

# S I M P L E

# MORE SCIENCE EXPERIMENTS

By Q. L. Pearce

Illustrated by Leo Abbett

LOWELL HOUSE JUVENILE

LOS ANGELES

*NTC/Contemporary Publishing Group*

## NOTE TO THE READER:

Many of the experiments in *60 Super Simple More Science Experiments* may require the use of a measuring cup, measuring spoons, a ruler, or a clock. These items are not listed under What You'll Need, unless they are needed for a specific purpose other than measuring.

*To my morale officers: Shiloh, Chatelet, and Lakota*
—Q. L. P.

*Special thanks to the students of Mrs. Zimmerman's class at Condit Elementary School, for their suggestions, research, and assistance with these experiments. Thank you Dusten, Caitlin, Sean, Amy, Nicole, Katie, A. J., Ivy, Michael, Stratton, Kelly, Arnold, Laura, Ross, Nadeen, Connie, Eric, Brennan, Bobby, and Daniel.*
—Q. L. P.

Published by Lowell House
A division of NTC/Contemporary Publishing Group, Inc.
4255 West Touhy Avenue, Lincolnwood (Chicago), Illinois 60712 U.S.A.

Managing Director and Publisher: Jack Artenstein
Director of Publishing Services: Rena Copperman
Editorial Director: Brenda Pope-Ostrow
Editor: Joanna Siebert
Typesetter: Carolyn Wendt
Cover Designer: Treesha Runnells Vaux

Lowell House books can be purchased at special discounts when ordered in bulk for premiums and special sales. Contact Customer Service at the address above, or call 1-800-323-4900.

Printed and bound in the United States of America

Library of Congress Catalog Card Number: 99-73108

ISBN: 0-7373-0233-X

10 9 8 7 6 5 4 3 2

# CONTENTS

1. Now You See It . . . . . . . . . . . . . . . 4

2. Balloon Business . . . . . . . . . . . . . 5

3. It's a Stretch . . . . . . . . . . . . . . . 6

4. Look, No Hands!. . . . . . . . . . . . . 8

5. Keeping Cool . . . . . . . . . . . . . . 10

6. Fill or Spill. . . . . . . . . . . . . . . . 12

7. Raising the Roof . . . . . . . . . . . . 13

8. The Big Split . . . . . . . . . . . . . . 14

9. Mix It Up. . . . . . . . . . . . . . . . . 16

10. Clouds of Color . . . . . . . . . . . . 17

11. Exceptional Egg . . . . . . . . . . . . 18

12. Up Periscope . . . . . . . . . . . . . . 20

13. Spice It Up . . . . . . . . . . . . . . . 22

14. On and On . . . . . . . . . . . . . . . 23

15. Around It Goes . . . . . . . . . . . . 24

16. High and Dry . . . . . . . . . . . . . 25

17. Going Up. . . . . . . . . . . . . . . . . 26

18. Don't Waste Your Breath. . . . . . . . 27

19. Take a Sip . . . . . . . . . . . . . . . . 28

20. Huff and Puff . . . . . . . . . . . . . . 29

21. Wave the Flag . . . . . . . . . . . . . 30

22. It's a Bang . . . . . . . . . . . . . . . . 32

23. Hello, Hello. . . . . . . . . . . . . . . 34

24. Say That Again . . . . . . . . . . . . . 35

25. Round and Round. . . . . . . . . . . . 36

26. It's a Snap . . . . . . . . . . . . . . . . 38

27. Push Comes to Shove . . . . . . . . . 39

28. Free Fall. . . . . . . . . . . . . . . . . . 40

29. In Orbit . . . . . . . . . . . . . . . . . 41

30. Going Nowhere. . . . . . . . . . . . . 42

31. On the Move . . . . . . . . . . . . . . 43

32. Here Comes the Sun. . . . . . . . . . 44

33. Going, Going, Gone . . . . . . . . . . 45

34. You've Been Fingered . . . . . . . . . 46

35. Get the Point. . . . . . . . . . . . . . 48

36. Every Beat of the Heart. . . . . . . . 49

37. Bridging the Gap. . . . . . . . . . . . 50

38. Have a Seat . . . . . . . . . . . . . . . 52

39. Shall We Dance? . . . . . . . . . . . . 53

40. The Pressure Is On . . . . . . . . . . 54

41. Bubble Up . . . . . . . . . . . . . . . . 55

42. Let It Rain . . . . . . . . . . . . . . . . 56

43. From Dark to Light . . . . . . . . . . 57

44. Air Power. . . . . . . . . . . . . . . . . 58

45. South Paw . . . . . . . . . . . . . . . . 59

46. The Sound of Music . . . . . . . . . . 60

47. Positive Attraction . . . . . . . . . . . 61

48. Water Power . . . . . . . . . . . . . . . 62

49. Phantom Colors . . . . . . . . . . . . 64

50. Metal Image. . . . . . . . . . . . . . . 65

51. Fluid Flow . . . . . . . . . . . . . . . . 66

52. What Time Is It? . . . . . . . . . . . . 68

53. Messed-Up Music. . . . . . . . . . . . 70

54. In the Eye of the Beholder . . . . . . 71

55. Crazy Colors . . . . . . . . . . . . . . 72

56. Drip, Drip, Drip. . . . . . . . . . . . . 74

57. Off Track . . . . . . . . . . . . . . . . 76

58. Twinkle, Twinkle, Little Star . . . . . 77

59. Follow That Star . . . . . . . . . . . . 78

60. Puffed Up . . . . . . . . . . . . . . . . 80

# NOW YOU
........................................................................
# SEE IT . . .

*A full glass of water has plenty of empty space in it. You can prove this amazing fact by mixing up a salty solution.*

## WHAT YOU'LL NEED
**• small drinking glass • water • salt • straw**

## DIRECTIONS

❶ Fill the glass to the rim with room temperature water.

❷ Very slowly, pour 2 tablespoons salt into the water. Stir the water with the straw until all the salt dissolves.

❸ Continue adding salt to the water using the tablespoon, stirring carefully each time, until the water finally spills over the edge. How many tablespoons of salt are you able to fit in the glass?

## WHAT'S GOING ON?

Molecules are tiny units of matter. Matter can take three different forms—solid, liquid, or gas. In a solid, molecules are slow-moving and packed tightly together. In a liquid, they are farther apart. In a gas, molecules are even farther apart than those in a liquid. Although you can't see it, there is plenty of empty space between the molecules in a glass of water. As you stir in the salt, it dissolves, or disappears, into the liquid, filling in the spaces. This forms a solution. A solution is what results when a solute (the material that dissolves—in this case, the salt) is combined with a solvent (what the material dissolves in—in this case, the water).

---

### Something Extra

Do you think the outcome of this experiment would be different if you changed the temperature of the water? Try it again using very cold water, then try it using hot water.

---

# BALLOON BUSINESS

What happens when air under pressure is suddenly released? Burst a balloon and you'll find out! But does a balloon have to burst? This experiment in properties of matter will help you find the answer.

## WHAT YOU'LL NEED
• two balloons • sharp pin • clear tape

## DIRECTIONS

❶ Blow up one balloon and tie the end closed. Stick the inflated balloon with the pin and observe what happens.

❷ Blow up the second balloon and tie the end closed.

❸ Tear off a 1-inch-long piece of tape and stick it onto the balloon. Be sure to smooth down the tape so it is flat.

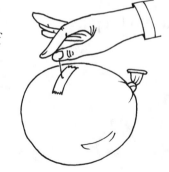

❹ Stick the pin through the center of the tape. What happens this time?

## WHAT'S GOING ON?
One of the properties of matter is stretchiness, or flexibility. The rubber that the balloon is made of is stretchy. When it is completely filled with air, it is stretched to its limit. This makes the rubber weak. It cannot stretch any farther without breaking. When you stick the first balloon with the pin, the air rushes out through the hole, tearing the weakened material as it goes. However, the tape on the second balloon is not stretched and remains strong. The air in this balloon leaks out slowly through the hole in the tape without it being torn. This makes the balloon deflate slowly.

# 3

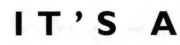

# IT'S A
# STRETCH

*Matter usually expands when it gets hotter, but with this experiment, the properties of matter might just surprise you.*

## WHAT YOU'LL NEED
• **12 thick books** • **pencil** • **small toy** • **large rubber band** • **hair dryer**

## DIRECTIONS

**❶** Stack all the books except one on a flat surface. Lay the pencil on the edge of the top book so half of it extends over the flat surface. Place the last book on top of the pencil to keep it securely in place.

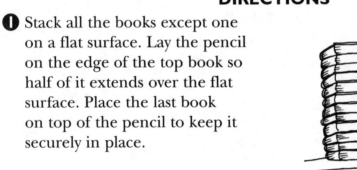

**❷** Attach the toy to the rubber band, as shown. Loop the other end of the rubber band over the pencil.

**❸** Look at how the experiment is set up. The toy should be barely touching the flat surface. If it is not, move the pencil up or down between another pair of books in the stack.

**4** Now turn on the hair dryer to a warm or hot setting. (For safety reasons, do not use the hair dryer near water.) Hold the hair dryer 1 or 2 inches from the rubber band and move it up and down so the air warms the entire rubber band. What happens to the toy?

## WHAT'S GOING ON?

Matter is any physical thing that takes up space or has weight. Everything around you—even air—is made up of matter. Matter has certain characteristics, or properties. Most types of matter expand when heated, but rubber is unusual. It contracts, rather than expands, when you warm it up. When you heat the rubber band with the hair dryer, it contracts slightly, lifting up the toy.

# LOOK, NO HANDS!

*The string in this experiment acts sort of like an ice magnet—but it's not magnetism at work here, it's the melting point of the ice.*

## WHAT YOU'LL NEED
• small glass bowl • water • ice cube • 4-inch-long piece of string • salt

## DIRECTIONS

❶ Fill the glass bowl nearly to the top with water. Place an ice cube into the water.

❷ Hold the string at one end and drape the other end across the ice cube. Sprinkle a pinch of salt around the string on the ice cube.

❸ Count slowly to 10, then pull up on the string to lift the ice cube out of the water.

# WHAT'S GOING ON?

Fresh water freezes at 32° Fahrenheit. Salt water freezes at a lower temperature, about 28.6° Fahrenheit. This happens because the molecules of salt that dissolve in the water interfere with the freezing process. By sprinkling salt on the ice cube, you lower its melting point and cause the ice around the string to melt slightly. The fresh water under the string quickly turns back to ice again, freezing the string in place. Now it is no problem to lift the ice cube out of the water.

## Something Extra

People often put salt on sidewalks and roads when the weather is very cold. Because salt water freezes at a lower temperature, sprinkling salt on fresh snow and ice causes it to melt. The melted snow and ice turns to water, making it much easier and safer for people and cars to get around. To test out this idea, use the plastic tops from two margarine containers. Put a thin layer of water on each top. Sprinkle salt on one top. Place them both in the freezer, keeping track of which top has salt water and which top has fresh water. Take out both tops after 1 hour. Tilt one side of a top up slightly and try to slide a penny across it. Do the same with the other top. Which top is more slippery?

# KEEPING
# COOL

*We keep food or drinks in an ice chest or cooler to prevent them from getting warm. But how does an ice chest work? Find out with this experiment.*

## WHAT YOU'LL NEED

• bucket • water • clay flowerpot • shallow bowl (large enough to stand the clay pot in)
• cold can of soda • small, flat stone

## DIRECTIONS

❶ Fill the bucket with cool water. Soak the flowerpot in the bucket for at least 30 minutes.

❷ Fill the shallow bowl with cool water.

❸ Place the can of soda in the center of the bowl.

**4** Place the flowerpot upside down in the bowl so it covers the can. If the flowerpot has one, cover the opening on the bottom with a small stone.

**5** Leave your "refrigerator" in a sunny spot. Check it after 30 minutes. Is your soda still cold? How about after an hour? How long does the soda stay cold?

## WHAT'S GOING ON?

When you soak the flowerpot in water, it absorbs, or holds, some of the water, making the flowerpot slightly damp. Eventually this water evaporates, or turns into a gas called water vapor, and moves into the air carrying away heat with it in the process. There is less heat inside the clay pot, so the soda remains cool. Because the flowerpot is in a bowl of water, the clay continues to absorb water. The evaporation process continues until all the water in the bowl is used up and the clay is dry. Once that happens, the flowerpot absorbs the heat energy and the soda begins to warm up.

# FILL OR

......................................................................................

# SPILL

*When matter gets cold, it usually contracts, or gets smaller. This experiment will prove that water is an exception to the rule.*

## WHAT YOU'LL NEED

**• ice cube • small drinking glass • water**

## DIRECTIONS

❶ Place an ice cube into the glass.

❷ Fill the glass to the rim with water. What does the ice cube do?

❸ Put the glass in a sunny location. Observe the glass of water as the ice melts. What happens?

## WHAT'S GOING ON?

Water, a type of matter, has some unusual properties. Unlike most things that get smaller, or contract, when frozen, water expands and becomes less dense. Density is the amount of matter squeezed into a given space. The more dense something is, the heavier it is. Because water expands and becomes less dense when it freezes, the ice cube is lighter than the water around it. It floats above the surface of the water. You may think that when the ice melts, the water level will also rise above the surface of the glass. However, when the ice cube melts, the water actually takes up less space than the ice cube does. The water level stays the same even with the additional water from the melted ice cube.

# RAISING THE ROOF

*During the last Ice Age, huge sheets of ice rearranged the landscape. Can ice really be that powerful? This experiment will give you a clue.*

## WHAT YOU'LL NEED

• empty plastic pint-size juice bottle • water • aluminum foil

## DIRECTIONS

❶ Fill the bottle to the top with water.

❷ Loosely cover the opening of the bottle with a square of aluminum foil.

❸ Place the bottle in the freezer. Check it after 24 hours. What happens to the aluminum foil?

## WHAT'S GOING ON?

Water expands when it freezes. At the beginning of this experiment, the water is confined within the bottle. As the water freezes, it pushes up through the bottle opening, lifting the aluminum foil cap with it. Imagine what the Earth must have been like during the last Ice Age, as rivers of ice, called glaciers, expanded across the land, carving out valleys and creating hills.

---

### Something Extra

What do you think would happen if you tried to keep the aluminum foil in place? Try the experiment again, but this time secure the foil with a rubber band.

---

# 8

# THE BIG SPLIT

**ADULT HELP REQUIRED**

*You use electricity every time you turn on a light. You can also use electricity to cause a chemical change.*

## WHAT YOU'LL NEED
• drinking glass • water • 1 teaspoon salt • spoon • two 4-inch pieces of electrical wire
• dry cell battery • two pencils, sharpened at both ends
• 2-inch-square piece of posterboard

## DIRECTIONS

❶ Fill the glass three-quarters full with water, and stir in 1 teaspoon salt.

❷ Have an adult strip about ½ inch of insulation from each end of the two pieces of wire. Attach one end of each piece to the battery, as shown on page 15.

❸ Poke the two pencils halfway through the posterboard about 1 inch apart. Attach the loose ends of each wire to one end of each pencil. Make sure the wires are touching the pencil lead.

**4** Rest the posterboard on top of the glass so the other ends of the pencil are in the salt water. Now observe the reaction.

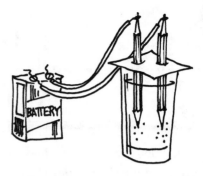

## WHAT'S GOING ON?

An electric current is a flow of electricity that passes easily through materials called conductors. The pencil lead is made from graphite, which is a good conductor of electricity. Water is made up of hydrogen and oxygen—$H_2O$. By passing an electric current from the battery through the salt water between two electrodes (the pencils), you split the $H_2O$ into its two parts, hydrogen and oxygen gas. The gas collects as bubbles on the two pencil tips in the water.

# 9

# MIX

## IT UP

*Oil and water don't mix—or do they? Try this demonstration to find out some of the characteristics of immiscible (im-MIS-ih-bul) liquids.*

## WHAT YOU'LL NEED

• ½ cup water • glass jar with lid • blue food coloring • spoon • ½ cup oil • dishwashing liquid

## DIRECTIONS

❶ Pour the water into the jar. Add 3 drops of blue food coloring to the water, then stir with the spoon. Next, slowly add the oil. Put the lid on the jar and allow it to remain undisturbed for 10 minutes. What happens to the oil and water?

❷ Shake the jar, then set it down and allow it to remain undisturbed for another 10 minutes. What happens?

❸ Now add 1 teaspoon dishwashing liquid to the jar. With the lid on, shake the jar again. Do the oil and water behave differently now?

❹ Allow the fluids to remain undisturbed for 1 hour. Do clear layers form?

## WHAT'S GOING ON?

Immiscible liquids are liquids that are different from each other and will not mix together. The layers of oil and water blend when you shake the jar, then quickly separate and form two layers. Dishwashing liquid is a detergent that breaks up oil. Once the dishwashing liquid is added to the jar, the oil forms tiny droplets that temporarily become suspended in the water. If you were to wash greasy dishes in water alone, the grease would resist being rinsed away. Adding detergent to the dishwater breaks up the grease into droplets. It becomes suspended in the water long enough to be rinsed down the drain.

# CLOUDS

# OF COLOR

*Which is heavier, warm water or cold water? This experiment on density will help you find the answer.*

## WHAT YOU'LL NEED

• small container, such as a film canister or empty aspirin bottle
• cold water • food coloring, any color • freezer • glass quart jar or 32-ounce beaker
• warm water • aluminum foil • rubber band • sharpened pencil

## DIRECTIONS

❶ Fill the small container with cold water, then add a few drops of food coloring. Place the container in the freezer for 10 minutes.

❷ Fill the quart jar or beaker to the rim with warm water.

❸ Remove the container from the freezer. Cover the open top of the container with aluminum foil and secure it with a rubber band. Use the pencil to poke a small hole in the center of the foil.

❹ Moving quickly, flip the container upside down and hold it so the hole is just below the surface of the water in the quart jar or beaker.

❺ Gently tap the bottom of the container.

## WHAT'S GOING ON?

The density of an object or substance is the amount it weighs in relation to the amount of space it takes up. There are more molecules in the cold water than there are in the same amount of warm water. Therefore, the cold water is more dense, or heavier, than the warm water. The cold water sinks through the warm water in colorful rings as you tap on the container.

# EXCEPTIONAL
## EGG

*Try this experiment on density to determine whether salt water or fresh water is heavier.*

### WHAT YOU'LL NEED

• two drinking glasses • water • two raw eggs • 5 tablespoons salt • spoon

### DIRECTIONS

**1** Fill the first glass halfway with water. Gently place an egg in the water. What happens to the egg?

**2** Fill the second glass halfway with water. Add the salt to the water and stir. Gently place an egg into the salt water. What happens this time?

**3** Carefully remove the eggs from both glasses without spilling any water. Slowly pour the fresh water into the glass of salt water until the glass is full. Leave the glass undisturbed for 10 minutes.

**4** Carefully place one egg into the full glass.

# WHAT'S GOING ON?

The density of an object or substance is the amount of matter it contains in relation to the amount of space it takes up. Salt water is more dense than fresh water because there's salt in the water. The egg floats in the salt water but does not float in the fresh water. The egg is more dense than fresh water, so it sinks. But the egg is not as dense as the salt water, so it floats. When you combine the glasses of water, the fresh water floats on top of the salt water. The egg sinks through the layer of fresh water but floats on the salt layer, becoming suspended in the middle of the glass.

---

### Something Extra

Does a hard-boiled egg have a different density than a raw egg? Try this experiment again and compare the density of a raw egg to a hard-boiled one.

---

# U P
# P E R I S C O P E

### ADULT HELP REQUIRED

*Air is lighter than water, which is why this model submarine works so well. You'll need some adult help to make it seaworthy.*

## WHAT YOU'LL NEED

• knife • 1-liter soda bottle • masking tape • four quarters • flexible drinking straw
• modeling clay • large plastic tub or bathtub • water

## DIRECTIONS

❶ Ask an adult to cut three pea-sized holes in the side of the soda bottle.

❷ Tape the quarters near the holes but do not cover them. The weight of the quarters will keep that side of the bottle underwater.

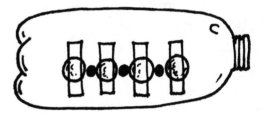

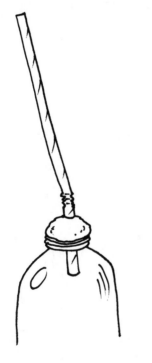

❸ Slip one end of the straw into the bottle through the opening, then seal the area around the straw with modeling clay. This is your submarine.

❹ Fill the tub with water. Dunk the submarine into the tub. It will fill with water and sink to the bottom.

**5** Blow hard into the straw. What happens to the submarine?

### WHAT'S GOING ON?

Air is lighter than water. When the submarine is filled with water, it sinks. When you blow into the straw, you fill the submarine with air, which pushes the water out. When it is filled with air instead of water, the submarine becomes lighter and rises to the surface. Two things cannot occupy the same space at the same time. Water cannot reenter the air-filled submarine as long as the straw is above water.

# S P I C E
# I T  U P

*Mixing salt and pepper together is easy. Separating them again is nearly impossible—unless you use static electricity!*

## WHAT YOU'LL NEED

• salt • pepper • shallow dish or saucer • wool scarf • plastic comb

## DIRECTIONS

❶ Sprinkle some salt and pepper onto a dish or saucer. Use your fingers to thoroughly mix them.

❷ Rub the wool scarf all over the plastic comb.

❸ Slowly move the plastic comb about ¼ inch above the dish. What happens?

## WHAT'S GOING ON?

Atoms are made up of very tiny particles. Some of these particles, called protons and electrons, have a property called charge. Protons have a positive charge. Electrons have a negative charge. Like charges (those that are the same) repel, or push each other away. Unlike charges (those that are different from each other) attract, or pull toward each other. When an atom has equal numbers of protons and electrons, the charges cancel each other out, and the atom is neutral. When you rub the comb with the wool scarf, you "knock" electrons off the atoms in the wool. They stick to the atoms in the comb. This creates static electricity, a buildup of charge on the surface of the comb. The salt and pepper are both attracted to the comb, but pepper is lighter than salt, so it is picked up first.

# ON
# AND ON

*Energy cannot be lost or created, but it can be changed into another form—as you can see with this demonstration of mechanical energy.*

## WHAT YOU'LL NEED

• **heavy book** • **table** • **pencil** • **20 inches of lightweight string** • **tape** • **two large marbles**

## DIRECTIONS

❶ Place the book on the edge of a table. Tuck the end of the pencil under the book so it sticks out over the table's edge.

❷ Center the string over the end of the pencil and tie it in place.

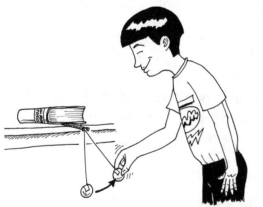

❸ Tape a marble to each end of the string. The two marbles should be perfectly even.

❹ Stand to the side, pull back the marble closest to you, and release it.

## WHAT'S GOING ON?

There are different types of energy. In this experiment, kinetic energy, the energy of motion, is transferred to the first marble when you pull it back and release it. In turn, that marble transfers energy to the second marble, causing it to swing out and back, hitting the first marble again. This continues, but with each collision some of the energy is converted to heat and sound energy. Once the kinetic energy is completely converted to heat and sound, the movement stops.

# AROUND
# IT GOES

*Knowledge of science can often make work easier. Here's an example.*

## WHAT YOU'LL NEED

• two large books • clean, unopened 1-gallon paint can • eight marbles

## DIRECTIONS

❶ Stack the books on top of the paint can. Try to turn the books in a circle. Remove the books.

❷ Place eight evenly spaced marbles around the rim of the paint can.

❸ Center the books on top of the marbles. Try to turn the books in a circle. Is it easier this time?

## WHAT'S GOING ON?

Friction is the resistance between materials that are sliding past each other. The friction between the books and the paint can makes it difficult to turn the books. Ball bearings are round balls that roll between moving parts. They roll easily and keep the moving parts separate, reducing friction. The marbles in this experiment act as ball bearings to reduce the friction between the books and the paint can, making the job easier.

# H I G H

# A N D   D R Y

*You can't see the air around you, but this experiment will show that it takes up space.*

## WHAT YOU'LL NEED

• tall plastic tub or bucket • water • handkerchief • small drinking glass • towel

## DIRECTIONS

❶ Fill the tub or bucket with water.

❷ Stuff the handkerchief into the bottom of the glass. Be sure it is wedged firmly in place.

❸ Turn the glass straight upside down and quickly push it to the bottom of the tub or bucket. Be sure to keep the glass straight and don't tilt it as you put it into the water. Pull the glass straight up out of the water. Dry your hands with a towel, then pull the handkerchief out of the glass. Is it wet or dry?

## WHAT'S GOING ON?

The handkerchief isn't the only thing in the glass. The glass is also full of air. When you push the glass straight down into the water, the air inside it becomes trapped. Since two substances can't occupy the same space at the same time, the trapped air keeps out the water. That is why the handkerchief stays completely dry.

---

### Something Extra

Try the experiment again, but this time hold the glass so it is slightly tilted. Is the handkerchief dry this time? Why or why not?

---

# GOING
# UP

*Can you fill a glass with water when it is upside down? You can by using air pressure.*

## WHAT YOU'LL NEED

• **tub or bucket** • **water** • **small drinking glass**

## DIRECTIONS

**❶** Fill the tub with water.

**❷** Place the glass upside down in the tub of water. Tilt the glass so it fills with water.

**❸** Holding the glass at the base, lift it straight up, keeping the rim underwater.

## WHAT'S GOING ON?

When you lift up the glass, the water level in the glass is much higher than the water level in the tub. Although you cannot feel it, air pushes on everything all the time. This is called air pressure. Air pressure is pushing down on the water in the tub. It actually pushes down with enough force to move the water level up in the glass. There is no air inside the glass to push the water down, so the water continues to fill the glass, even as it rises.

---

### Something Extra

Continue with this experiment. Lift the rim of the glass above the water's surface. What happens to the water? Why?

---

# DON'T WASTE YOUR BREATH

*Blowing a small piece of paper into an empty bottle sounds easy. With air pressure working against you, it isn't as simple as it sounds.*

## WHAT YOU'LL NEED

• empty ½-liter soda bottle • table • 3-inch-square piece of paper

## DIRECTIONS

❶ Place the bottle on its side with the mouth of the bottle near the edge of the table.

❷ Crumple the paper into a tight ball and set it just inside the mouth of the bottle.

❸ Stand in front of the table. Try to blow the paper into the bottle. Can you do it?

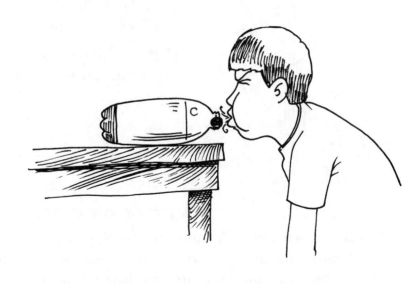

## WHAT'S GOING ON?

When you blow at the mouth of the bottle, more air enters the bottle, increasing the air pressure (the pushing force of air) inside. The air then moves to a place where the air pressure is lower—outside the bottle. The paper is pushed out with the air instead of being blown inside.

# TAKE
# A SIP

*Air pressure makes a straw work, or in this case, not work.*

## WHAT YOU'LL NEED
• **drinking glass** • **water** • **two straws**

## DIRECTIONS

❶ Fill the glass with water.

❷ Hold the two straws near each other, with one straw in the water and the other one outside the glass.

❸ Place the ends of both straws into your mouth. Try to take a sip of water.

## WHAT'S GOING ON?

Normally, when you suck through a straw, you lower the air pressure in your mouth. Since the air pressure is greater outside your mouth, water is pushed down in the glass, then up through the straw into your mouth. In this experiment, the air pressure in your mouth is not lowered because the second straw allows more air to enter. You should not be able to take a sip of water through either straw.

---

### Something Extra

Try covering the end of the straw outside the glass with your finger. Can you take a sip of water now? Why or why not?

---

# HUFF
## AND PUFF

*Some things are more difficult than they seem. This demonstration of the Bernoulli principle is a good example.*

## WHAT YOU'LL NEED
• Ping-Pong® ball • wide-mouthed funnel

## DIRECTIONS

**❶** Place the ball into the wide end of the funnel.

**❷** Tilt back your head and hold the small end of the funnel in your mouth. Blow a steady stream of air through it.

**❸** Now blow as hard as you can. Are you able to blow the ball out of the funnel?

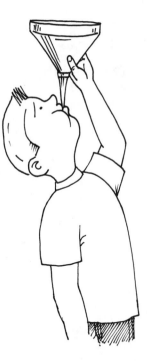

## WHAT'S GOING ON?

According to the Bernoulli principle, a stream of air creates borders of lower air pressure. When you blow air through the funnel, a pocket of low air pressure is created at the underside of the ball. The higher air pressure above the ball pushes down on it. The harder you blow, the more securely the ball stays nestled in the funnel.

# WAVE
# THE FLAG

*It's easy to use a breath of air to make a small paper flag wave. In this experiment, you can even do it with a tap of your finger.*

## WHAT YOU'LL NEED

• tape • two 2-inch-wide circles cut from a plastic sandwich bag
• cardboard tube from a roll of bathroom tissue • toothpick
• 1-inch-square of lightweight tissue paper • scissors • clay

## DIRECTIONS

**1** Tape the plastic circles over each end of the cardboard tube.

**2** Using the toothpick, make a small hole in the plastic on one end.

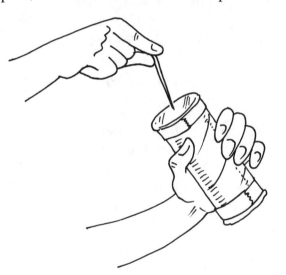

**3** Attach the tissue to one end of the toothpick with tape. Use the scissors to make small cuts across the tissue to create strips. This is your flag.

**4** Press a pea-sized ball of clay onto a flat surface and stick the other end of the toothpick into it so the flag stands up.

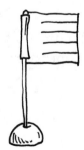

**5** Hold the tube about 1 inch from the flag, with the hole in the plastic facing it. Tap the plastic on the other end of the tube with your finger. What happens?

## WHAT'S GOING ON?

When you tap the plastic, air molecules within the tube vibrate, or move. The vibration passes through other air molecules in waves as the molecules bump into each other. A puff of air is forced through the tiny hole in the plastic, making the tissue flag flutter slightly.

# IT'S A BANG

*You may not be able to see air, but you can certainly hear it with this air trapper.*

## WHAT YOU'LL NEED

- **12- by 16-inch piece of paper**
**(newspaper, construction paper, or wrapping paper will work)**

## DIRECTIONS

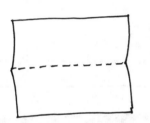

❶ Fold the paper in half lengthwise. Make a sharp crease, then open it again.

❷ Fold each of the four corners toward the center. Then fold the paper in half again.

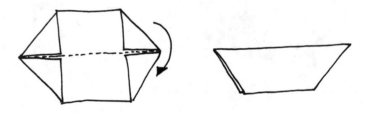

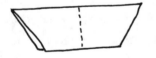

❸ Fold the paper in half so the two pointed ends meet. Then open it again.

❹ Fold the two pointed ends down so they form a triangle.

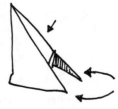

**5** Hold the air trapper by the two "wings" and snap it downward. What do you hear?

## WHAT'S GOING ON?

As you snap the air trapper down, you force air out of the way. What you hear as a loud bang is the moving air.

# HELLO,
# HELLO

*Here's a way for you and a friend to transfer a cupful of sound from one place to another.*

## WHAT YOU'LL NEED

• sharpened pencil • two paper drinking cups • 10 feet of string

## DIRECTIONS

**1** Use the pencil to make a small hole in the center of the bottom of each cup.

**2** Push one end of the string through the hole in one cup. Tie a knot in the string so it won't pull through the cup. The knot should be inside the cup.

**3** Push one end of the string through the hole in the second cup. Tie a knot in the string so it won't pull through the cup. Again, the knot should be inside the cup.

**4** Give a friend one of the cups and hold the other one. Stand far enough apart so the string is taut, or tight. Hold the cup to your ear while your friend speaks in a normal tone into his or her cup. What do you hear?

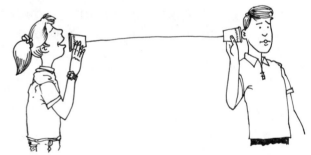

## WHAT'S GOING ON?

Sound is actually waves of vibrations, or movements. When the sound waves reach your ears, your brain interprets them as sound. Most often, you hear sound as it moves through air. But sound waves travel easily through certain solids, such as the string you use in this experiment. It might be hard to hear your friend's voice if he or she were to speak in a normal tone from 10 feet away. But with the string, you can hear sound well.

# SAY THAT AGAIN

*With this homemade megaphone, you can focus the sound of your voice so your friends will hear you loud and clear.*

## WHAT YOU'LL NEED

• 8½- by 11-inch sheet of paper • tape

## DIRECTIONS

❶ Roll the paper into a cone shape, leaving an opening for your mouth. Use tape to secure the cone.

❷ Ask a friend to stand at least 20 feet away. Count to 10 out loud in a normal tone of voice.

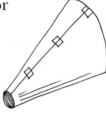

❸ Aim the large end of the cone toward your friend. Hold the other end near your mouth. Count to 10 again, still using a normal tone of voice. Is it easier for your friend to hear you?

## WHAT'S GOING ON?

Sound waves are made by vibrations, or movements. Without the megaphone, the vibrations would have moved through the air in all directions. The cone shape of the paper megaphone concentrates the sound so it doesn't spread out. The megaphone directs the sound vibrations toward your friend, making it easier for him or her to hear you.

---

### Something Extra

Can the megaphone help you hear your friend more clearly? Hold the small end of the megaphone near (but not in) your ear. Point the wide end of the cone toward your friend as he or she speaks. Is it easier to hear what is being said? Why?

---

# ROUND
............................................................
# AND ROUND

**ADULT HELP REQUIRED**

*If you take a mechanical toy apart, you're likely to find gears inside. Try this demonstration to see how gears work.*

## WHAT YOU'LL NEED

• knife • large potato • 12 toothpicks • sharpened pencil • two plastic drinking straws

## DIRECTIONS

❶ Ask an adult to cut two ½-inch slices from the center of the potato.

❷ Stick six evenly-spaced toothpicks deep into the edge of each slice.

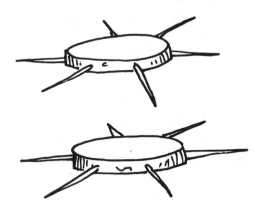

❸ Use the pencil to poke a hole into the center of the first slice. The hole should be slightly bigger than the straw.

❹ Poke a straw through the center of the second slice. Make sure it fits tightly.

**❺** Place the first potato slice on a flat surface. Place one end of a straw in the hole to hold the piece loosely in place on the surface. With your other hand, hold the straw in the second slice (or gear) horizontally so the toothpicks interlock with the toothpicks of the first slice (or gear). Turn the straw. What happens to the slice that is on the flat surface?

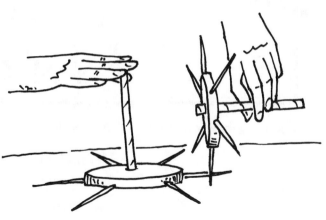

## WHAT'S GOING ON?

In this experiment, the potato slices act as gears. The toothpicks act as the teeth in the gears. When you turn one of the straws, the second gear moves in a circular motion. The interlocking teeth cause the gear on the table to move as well, even though you aren't touching it directly.

---

### Something Extra

What happens when you reverse the direction of the second gear? Can you design a demonstration using three gears?

---

# IT'S A
# SNAP

*Can you break a wooden match with the tips of your fingers? Try it out.*

## WHAT YOU'LL NEED
• **wooden match**

## DIRECTIONS

❶ Hold your hand out in front of you, palm down.

❷ Place a match across the back of your middle finger at the first knuckle, near the fingertip. Slip the fingers on either side of your middle finger over the top of the match to hold it in place.

❸ Try to snap the match by pushing up with your middle finger. Can you do it?

❹ If you can't snap the match, move it to a new spot along your middle finger. Does it work now?

## WHAT'S GOING ON?

A lever is a type of tool that is used to lift heavy weights. The effort you make to lift the load is called the force. The closer the force is to the fulcrum (the point on which the lever turns), the easier it will be to succeed. In this experiment, your finger is the lever and the knuckle at the base of the finger (nearest your hand) is the fulcrum. With the match at your first knuckle, the effort is concentrated near your fingertip, not near the knuckle where you lift your finger—the fulcrum. You can't break the match this way. You must move the match closer to your hand to snap it.

# PUSH COMES TO SHOVE

*A broom handle can tear through a piece of tissue, can't it? This demonstration of the diversion of force might surprise you and prove the opposite.*

## WHAT YOU'LL NEED

• facial tissue • cardboard center from a roll of paper towels
• rubber band • fine sand • broom

## DIRECTIONS

❶ Secure the tissue over one opening of the cardboard roll with a rubber band.

❷ Fill the cardboard roll halfway up with sand.

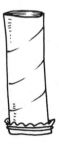

❸ Hold the roll in one hand, and try to push the broom handle through the sand and tissue.

## WHAT'S GOING ON?

You use a lot of force when you push down on the broom handle, but only a small amount reaches the tissue. As you push down with the broomstick, the grains of sand in the roll bang into each other, sending the force in many different directions. By the time it reaches the tissue, there is little direct force left and the tissue doesn't break.

39

# FREE FALL

*Because of gravity, what goes up must come down. Thanks to momentum, it doesn't have to come down in a straight line.*

## WHAT YOU'LL NEED

• old sock • sand • flat rock

## DIRECTIONS

❶ Fill the sock with sand, then tie the open end in a knot.

❷ Place the rock on the ground.

❸ Stand about 20 feet from the rock. Hold the sock out to one side. Run toward the rock as fast as you can. Try to drop it directly on the rock as you pass by. How close do you get to the rock?

## WHAT'S GOING ON?

It may take several tries to successfully hit the rock. The sock has momentum, which is the force produced by a moving body. Once something is moving, it takes an even stronger force to stop it or change its course. You are running when you drop the sock, so it has a forward momentum, or a forward motion. Gravity (a force that attracts objects toward the Earth's center) has to overcome the forward momentum of the sock. Even though gravity causes the sock to fall toward the ground, it does not drop down in a straight line. It still has a forward motion of its own, so it falls in a curved path and lands in front of the rock. In order to hit the target, you have to drop the sock just before you reach the rock. That takes practice!

# IN
# ORBIT

*It doesn't take much to keep satellites in orbit, just forward speed and centripetal force. This demonstration works best outdoors.*

## WHAT YOU'LL NEED

• **large bolt** • **3 feet of lightweight string** • **empty thread spool** • **roll of masking tape**

## DIRECTIONS

**1** Tie the bolt to one end of the string.

**2** Slip the other end of the string through the hole in the thread spool. Then tie it to the roll of masking tape.

**3** Hold the spool and masking tape in one hand while you spin the bolt over your head to get it going. Once it's spinning, drop the masking tape roll and let it hang freely. Hold the spool out in front of you. Move the spool in tight circles to keep the bolt going.

## WHAT'S GOING ON?

In this demonstration, the masking tape on the string represents centripetal force, or the force that draws an object toward the center as it moves in a circle. You give the bolt forward speed by swinging it in a big circle over your head. Forward speed keeps the bolt moving in an outward motion. Without a weight on the end of the string, the bolt would have pulled the string out of the spool and zoomed away. The weight of the masking tape roll pulls at the string and keeps the bolt from flying off. The force pulling the bolt toward the center (the weight of the masking tape) and the forward motion of the bolt balance each other out, keeping the bolt "in orbit."

# GOING
# NOWHERE

*Some satellites (objects that orbit the Earth) appear to stay in the same place high above the Earth. That is because they are in a geostationary orbit.*

## WHAT YOU'LL NEED

**• modeling clay • 12-inch piece of stiff wire • pencil**

## DIRECTIONS

❶ Divide the modeling clay into two balls. Make the first ball about the size of an orange. This represents the Earth. Make the second ball of clay the size of a large pea. This represents a satellite.

❷ Stick one end of the wire into the first ball and the other end of the wire into the second ball. Stick the pencil into the first ball, perpendicular to the wire.

❸ Turn the pencil around and around to move the first ball, or Earth. What happens to the second ball, the satellite?

## WHAT'S GOING ON?

The second ball, which represents a satellite, has to cover more distance as it moves. Therefore, it must move faster than the first ball (the Earth). Many objects have been sent into orbit around the Earth. A satellite settles into orbit when its forward speed (which makes it fly away from the planet) is balanced with the effect of gravity (which is the force causing it to fall toward the planet). The time a satellite takes to circle the planet depends on how far away it is from the planet. The closer it is to the planet, the stronger the effect of gravity, so its forward speed must be faster. Certain satellites must stay in orbit over a particular spot on Earth. These are called geostationary satellites. The Earth turns, or rotates, on its axis (an imaginary line that runs from the North Pole to the South Pole through the planet) once every 24 hours. Its rotational speed is about 1,000 miles per hour. To match the Earth's rotation and stay in orbit over one location on the equator, a satellite would have to be about 22,000 miles above the Earth.

# ON THE MOVE

*Planets and their moons move within the galaxy. But did you know that the galaxies are moving too? They are rushing away from each other. This demonstration will show how.*

## WHAT YOU'LL NEED

• **round balloon** • **black marker** • **cloth measuring tape** • **notebook** • **pencil**

## DIRECTIONS

❶ Blow up the balloon to about the size of a tennis ball. Hold the end closed with your fingers but don't tie it.

❷ Use the marker to write the numbers 1 to 20 anywhere on the surface of the balloon. Choose any 10 pairs of numbers and measure the distance between them with the measuring tape. Write your findings down in your notebook.

❸ Now blow up the balloon completely. Tie the end of the balloon closed. What happens to the numbers on the balloon?

❹ Check the distance between each pair of numbers measured before. Record the new measurements in your notebook. Are they different or the same as the measurements from before?

## WHAT'S GOING ON?

As you blow up the balloon, it expands, or moves outward, taking up more space. The distance between each number increases. Many astronomers believe the universe started with a single "explosion" called the Big Bang. As the galaxies formed, the force of the explosion sent them racing outward. They believe that the universe is still expanding and that the galaxies, like the numbers on the balloon, are moving away from each other.

# HERE COMES

# THE SUN

*To us, the Sun travels in a particular path across the sky. Here's a way to track its movement.*

## WHAT YOU'LL NEED

**• sharp-pointed black marker • 8½- by 11-inch piece of stiff white paper**
**• directional compass • shallow, clear glass bowl (at least 6 inches across)**

## DIRECTIONS

**1** Draw an X at the center of the paper with the marker. In the morning, set the paper in a sunny spot outside. Be sure to choose a spot that will be in the Sun all day. Place the compass on top of the X. Look at where the needle is pointing. Follow the direction of the needle to the edge of the paper, then write an N for north. At the opposite edge of the paper, write an S for south. On the left side of the paper, write a W for west, and on the right side of the paper, write an E for east. Remove the compass.

**2** Turn the bowl upside down on the paper. Make sure the X is under the center of the bowl. Hold the pen near the rim on one side of the bowl so the end of the pen's shadow touches the X on the paper. Draw a large dot on the glass at this spot.

**3** Draw another dot every hour until sunset. What path do the dots make?

## WHAT'S GOING ON?

When you draw the first dot, the Sun is low in the sky. The shadow of the pen is long and reaches the X even from near the rim of the bowl. As the Sun climbs higher in the sky, the shadow becomes shorter and you have to move the pen higher up the bowl to make it touch the X. At noon, when the Sun is almost directly above, the shadow is very short. As the Sun moves lower in the sky, the shadow is cast from the opposite side of the bowl. The line of dots that you draw follows the apparent path of the Sun in the daytime sky. The Sun seems to move from east to west, but the Sun isn't actually moving across the sky. Instead, the Earth is turning, or rotating on its axis, from west to east.

# G O I N G ,
# G O I N G ,   G O N E

*The environment is always changing. One of the forces at work is erosion.*

## WHAT YOU'LL NEED
• **three drinking glasses** • **water** • **three candy-coated chocolates, such as M&M's®**

## DIRECTIONS

❶ Fill two glasses with water. Leave the third empty.

❷ Place a candy in each glass. Set the glasses on a flat surface where they will not be disturbed.

❸ Pick up the first glass by the rim and swirl it in a circular motion for about 30 seconds. Do this every 10 minutes for 1 hour. Don't disturb the other glasses. What happens to the candies in each glass?

## WHAT'S GOING ON?

The candy in the first glass dissolves much more than the others do. When you swirl the glass around, molecules in the water bump into molecules in the candy and knock them off, so the candy dissolves faster. Although the candy in the second glass is dissolving as well, the process is slower because the water isn't moving. The candy in the third glass doesn't change. Water can have a similar effect on rocks and soil in the environment. Over time, moving water, such as rainwater or river water, erodes, or wears away, objects in its path.

---

### Something Extra
Would the effect be different if you changed the fluid in the experiment? Try it again using a solution of half water and half vinegar.

---

# YOU'VE BEEN

# FINGERED

*Is it true that no two people have the same fingerprints? You'll need at least 10 friends to help discover the answer.*

## WHAT YOU'LL NEED
• sharpened pencil • 11 8½- by 11-inch sheets of white paper
• clear tape • magnifying glass

## DIRECTIONS

❶ Rub the side of the pencil on the paper to make 20 one-inch-square areas of lead.

❷ Have a friend gently press his or her finger onto one area of pencil lead.

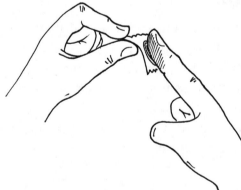

❸ Press a piece of tape onto your friend's fingertip to carefully lift the print. Stick the tape onto a clean piece of white paper. Write your friend's name under his or her print.

❹ Do the same thing with each friend, putting each print on a separate sheet of paper.

**5** Use the magnifying glass to study the pattern of each fingerprint. Do any of the prints look exactly the same? Can you pick out certain patterns that are similar from print to print?

## WHAT'S GOING ON?

Every person in the world has a unique set of fingerprints. Each person's fingerprints are made up of a particular combination of lines, loops, and curves. Although these patterns may be similar from person to person, they are never the same. Even the fingerprints of identical twins are different. When you study your friends' fingerprints, you see that they are all different, although some may be similar.

---

### Something Extra

Can you uncover fingerprints and match them to your friends? Offer each of your friends a glass of water, then line up the glasses on a table. Ask an adult for a cosmetic brush and some loose facial powder. Gently dust the glasses with powder and see if you can find any clear fingerprints. Can you figure out which glass belongs to which friend this way?

---

# GET THE
# POINT

*Is your upper arm or lower arm as sensitive as the tip of your finger? It's easy to get the point of this experiment. Ask a friend to help.*

## WHAT YOU'LL NEED
**• tape • two sharpened pencils • volunteer • notebook • pen**

## DIRECTIONS

❶ Tape the two pencils together. The tips need to be even, so rest them on a flat surface as you tape the pencils together. Don't let your volunteer see the two pencils taped together.

❷ Have your volunteer stretch out an arm and close his or her eyes.

❸ Lightly touch the pencil tips someplace on your volunteer's upper arm. Ask him or her to tell you how many pencils you are using, then record the answer in your notebook.

❹ Now do the same thing on your volunteer's lower arm. How many pencils does he or she feel this time?

❺ Try it on the tip of the person's index finger. Does it feel differently now?

## WHAT'S GOING ON?

The human skin has many nerve endings that sense heat, pain, and pressure. The brain receives this information, interprets it, then decides how to react. There are far more nerve endings in the fingertips than there are in the upper and lower arm. We constantly use our fingers to touch things and gather information about our environment, so it makes sense that they are more sensitive. For this reason, it is easier for your volunteer to feel both pencil tips on his or her index finger. The volunteer can feel the pressure of the pencils on his or her upper and lower arm, but cannot tell how many pencils there are.

# EVERY BEAT
# OF THE HEART

*A human heart beats a certain number of times every minute. You can use this stethoscope to listen to your own heart at work.*

## WHAT YOU'LL NEED

• **2 feet of ½-inch-wide plastic tubing (available at hardware or aquarium supply stores)**
• **two plastic funnels with ½-inch openings • watch or clock with a second hand**

## DIRECTIONS

❶ Slip one end of the tubing over the tip of a funnel, and slip the opposite end of the tubing over the tip of the second funnel.

❷ Sit in a quiet place. Press the wide end of one funnel against the center of your chest.

❸ Place the wide end of the other funnel against your ear. Relax, breathe regularly, and listen. Look at a watch or clock and count how many times your heart beats in 15 seconds. Multiply that number by four to find out how often your heart beats per minute.

## WHAT'S GOING ON?

As blood is pumped from the heart, it creates vibrations, or movements, that make sound waves. You cannot usually hear your own heart beating because the sound is very soft and the vibrations are muffled and scattered in all directions as they move through your body. In this experiment, the stethoscope directs the sound through the tubing and up to your ear, making it seem louder. When a child is sitting quietly, his or her heart beats 80 to 90 times per minute on average.

---

### Something Extra

Try the same experiment after running in place for 5 minutes. Is the number of times your heart beats different? Why?

---

# BRIDGING
................................................
# THE GAP

*Why don't arched bridges collapse in the middle? This bridge of books will explain how the center of gravity can safely bridge the gap.*

## WHAT YOU'LL NEED
• **two wood or metal chairs of equal size**
• **11 hardcover books (approximately 8½- by 11-inches or larger and ½- to 1-inch thick)**

## DIRECTIONS

**❶** Set up the chairs so they face each other. Leave about 1 foot of space between the front edges of the seats.

**❷** Carefully place a book on the seat of each chair so the short end sticks out about 1 inch over the edge.

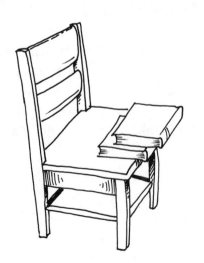

**❸** Place another book on top of each of these books. Each new book should extend about 1 inch or so over the edge of the book below it.

50

**❹** Continue to stack the books on top of each other this way.

**❺** Place the last book on top of both stacks.

## WHAT'S GOING ON?

Objects—and people, too—have a center of gravity, or the point at which they are balanced and stable. The lower the center of gravity is to its area of support, and the larger the area of support, the more in balance an object will be. As the bridge is built, the first level of books is supported securely by the chair with only an inch of book sticking out into the air. The second level of books is supported by the first layer of books. By the time you place the final book on top, it is supported by all the layers of books beneath it, with only a gap of 2 inches to cover. All the books are in balance.

---

### Something Extra

Try this experiment with fewer books. What is the fewest number of books you can use to make a stable bridge when the chairs are 1 foot apart? What is the greatest distance you can have between the chairs if you make a bridge using only three books?

---

# HAVE
............................................................
# A SEAT

*People have a center of gravity, and sometimes it can have some surprising effects.*

## WHAT YOU'LL NEED

• straight-backed wooden or metal chair

## DIRECTIONS

❶ Sit in the chair with your back straight, your arms crossed over your chest, and your feet flat on the floor.

❷ Try to stand up. What happens?

❸ Uncross your arms, lean forward, and try to stand up. Was the result different this time?

## WHAT'S GOING ON?

Gravity causes your body to fall toward the Earth. People and objects have a center of gravity, or the point at which they are balanced and stable. Your muscular and skeletal systems work together to maintain balance. When you are standing, your center of gravity is over your feet. When you sit up straight in a chair, your center of gravity is over your tailbone. The chair keeps you from falling to the ground. In this position, your leg muscles alone are not strong enough to work against the effect of Earth's gravity and lift you into a standing position. To stand, you have to shift your center of gravity back over your feet by moving your upper body forward.

# SHALL WE DANCE?

*Here is a fun example of your center of gravity working against you.*

## WHAT YOU'LL NEED
- door

## DIRECTIONS

❶ Open a door halfway. Stand up straight with your nose just touching the edge of the door and your feet on either side of it (the edge of the door should be about even with the tips of your toes).

❷ Try to lift your heels and rise onto your toes.

## WHAT'S GOING ON?

When you are standing flat on your feet, your center of gravity, or the point at which you are balanced and stable, is directly over your feet. In order to stand on your toes, you must shift your center of gravity by leaning forward. Normally, you would do this without thinking about it. This time you aren't able to rise onto your toes because you can't lean forward—the door is in your way.

---

### Something Extra

Where do you think the center of gravity on a yardstick might be? Balance a yardstick on top of both index fingers, placed at the 1- and 36-inch positions. Slide your fingers together until they meet, without dropping the yardstick. No matter how hard you try to change it, your fingers will always come together in the same place on the yardstick. That place is the only point at which the yardstick will be balanced and stable. That is its center of gravity.

---

# THE PRESSURE
# IS ON

*Watch a piece of wire pass through ice and still leave a solid block of ice behind. It's not magic, but pressure at work.*

## WHAT YOU'LL NEED

• 1½-inch-long piece of strong, thin wire • two large bolts
• bottle with a cork (such as a wine or vinegar bottle) • ice cube • refrigerator

## DIRECTIONS

❶ Twist one end of the wire around one bolt, and twist the other end of the wire around the second bolt.

❷ Place the bottle with the cork in it on a flat surface. Balance the ice cube on top of the cork.

❸ Drape the wire over the center of the ice cube so the bolts hang down on either side of the bottle.

❹ Put the bottle in the refrigerator and check it every 10 minutes. The wire will travel slowly through the ice cube all the way to the cork. How does the ice cube look?

## WHAT'S GOING ON?

The pressure from the wire melts the ice directly beneath it. The wire drops through the water, which refreezes behind it, leaving the ice cube in one piece above the wire.

# BUBBLE
# UP

*In this experiment, you can blow up a balloon using a chemical reaction.*

## WHAT YOU'LL NEED

• ½ cup vinegar • empty 12-ounce soda bottle • 1 tablespoon baking soda
• one square of toilet tissue • balloon

## DIRECTIONS

❶ Pour the vinegar into the soda bottle.

❷ Place the baking soda in the center of the tissue. Roll it into a tight packet and twist the ends closed.

❸ Drop the baking soda packet into the bottle. Quickly slip the balloon over the neck of the bottle and hold it in place.

## WHAT'S GOING ON?

A chemical reaction between the vinegar, an acid, and the baking soda, a base, causes carbon dioxide gas to form. The molecules that form the gas expand, or move farther apart, and take up more space than the molecules that make up the vinegar and baking soda. As the newly formed gas expands, it escapes into the balloon, blowing it up in the process.

---

### Something Extra

Once the balloon has stopped expanding, use duct tape to secure it in place on the bottle. Use plenty of tape to be sure that the gas does not escape through the opening. Observe the balloon for a while. Does it deflate? How or why could that happen?

---

# LET IT RAIN

*Where does water go when it evaporates? Check out this experiment to discover the answer.*

## WHAT YOU'LL NEED

• **two glass jars** • **water** • **marker** • **aluminum foil**

## DIRECTIONS

**1** Fill both jars halfway with water. Use the marker to make a line on each jar right at the water level.

**2** Cover the top of one of the jars with aluminum foil. Leave the other jar uncovered.

**3** Place both jars in a sunny location. Check and mark the water levels on each jar every hour.

## WHAT'S GOING ON?

The water in each jar begins to evaporate. It turns into water vapor, which you cannot see, in the air. As the water vapor from the open jar drifts away, the water level drops. The water vapor in the closed jar can't escape. It condenses, or forms into beads, on the foil and drips back into the jar. The water level in this jar remains almost the same.

# FROM DARK TO LIGHT

*Why do you feel warmer when you wear dark-colored clothes? Try this experiment on a sunny day and it will help you figure it out.*

## WHAT YOU'LL NEED

• four ice cubes • two plastic sandwich bags • 8½- by 11-inch sheet of black construction paper
• stapler • 8½- by 11-inch sheet of white construction paper

## DIRECTIONS

❶ Place two ice cubes into each sandwich bag.

❷ Fold the black construction paper in half around one sandwich bag. Staple the paper closed on two of the open sides to form a pocket.

❸ Fold the white construction paper in half around the other sandwich bag, then staple it closed on two of the open sides.

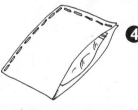

❹ Place both bags in a sunny spot outside. Check them every 10 minutes to see which ice cubes are melting faster.

## WHAT'S GOING ON?

Light and heat are two forms of energy. The Sun is a source of tremendous energy, some of which reaches the Earth as light and heat. Colors absorb, or take in, energy in different amounts. Colors also reflect, or bounce away, energy in different amounts. Black absorbs most of the energy, while white reflects it. Ice is the solid form of water. When heat is added, the ice melts and becomes liquid. Since the black absorbs more heat energy, the ice under the black paper melts faster. The white paper reflects much of the heat energy, keeping the ice cubes cooler, so they melt more slowly.

# AIR
......................................................
# POWER

*If you need assistance lifting a heavy object, this demonstration of the power of air pressure might help.*

## WHAT YOU'LL NEED
**• large balloon • table • 1-inch-thick book**

## DIRECTIONS

**1** Place the balloon on a table with the neck hanging over the edge.

**2** Place the book on top of the balloon.

**3** Try to blow air into the balloon. What happens?

## WHAT'S GOING ON?

When you blow into the balloon, you force air in and make the balloon expand, or get larger. At first it is hard to get air into the balloon because the pressure of gravity acting on the entire book (known as the book's weight) is greater than the pressure of the air in the balloon. As you blow in more air, you increase the pressure of the air inside the balloon until it is greater than the pressure of gravity acting on the book. Once you do that, the air pressure is able to lift the book.

# S O U T H
# P A W

*Is your pet right- or left-pawed? You'll need a cooperative animal helper to perform this experiment.*

## WHAT YOU'LL NEED
• pet treat • glass jar • masking tape • dog or cat

## DIRECTIONS

❶ Place the pet treat in the bottom of the jar.

❷ Place the jar on its side on the floor. Secure the jar to the floor with masking tape.

❸ Show your pet the treat and observe its behavior.

## WHAT'S GOING ON?

There are several theories, or ideas, for the reason people usually prefer one hand to the other, but there are no definite answers. Some scientists think it depends on which hand a person's parents used. Others say it depends on training. Still, even babies seem to use one hand more than the other. Just like people, animals may favor using a right or left paw. As you observe your pet trying to get the treat, you'll probably notice that it uses one paw more frequently. That will help you determine whether the pet is right- or left-pawed.

# THE SOUND
# OF MUSIC

*Sound vibrations travel at different speeds. The difference that we hear is known as pitch.*

## WHAT YOU'LL NEED
**• five drinking glasses (all the same size and shape) • water • wooden spoon**

## DIRECTIONS

❶ Place the five glasses in a row, with 1 inch of space between each one.

❷ Leave the first glass empty. Fill the second glass with 1 inch of water, the third glass with 2 inches of water, the fourth glass with 3 inches of water, and the fifth glass with 4 inches of water.

❸ Use the wooden spoon to gently tap on the side of each glass. Does each one make a different sound? Try to play a tune.

## WHAT'S GOING ON?

Sound is actually waves of vibrations. When you tap the glass, you make it vibrate, or move rapidly back and forth, creating sound waves. The number of vibrations per second is called the frequency of the sound. Pitch is a characteristic of sound, and it is a measure of frequency. A high frequency means a high pitch. Adding water to a glass changes the frequency and also the pitch. The glass without any water vibrates the most and has the highest pitch. The glass with the most water vibrates the least and has the lowest pitch.

# POSITIVE ATTRACTION

Static electricity can have some interesting effects on the surroundings, as you will see in this experiment.

## WHAT YOU'LL NEED
• plastic comb • wool or silk scarf • faucet

## DIRECTIONS

❶ Rub the comb on the scarf for about 30 seconds.

❷ Turn on the faucet so a thin stream of water is flowing.

❸ Hold the comb as near to the water as you can without actually touching it. What happens to the water?

## WHAT'S GOING ON?

Atoms are made up of smaller particles. Some of these particles, called protons and electrons, have a property called charge. When an atom has equal numbers of protons and electrons, the charges cancel each other out and the atom is neutral. Some atoms have a positive charge. Others have a negative charge. Like charges (those that are the same) repel, or push each other away, but unlike (different) charges attract or pull toward each other. By rubbing the comb with the scarf, you knock electrons off some of the atoms in the scarf. This creates static electricity, a buildup of charge on the surface of the comb. The stream of water is attracted to the comb and bends toward it.

# WATER
# POWER

*Be an engineer. Create your own working water wheel and imagine its many uses.*

## WHAT YOU'LL NEED

**• scissors • paper plate • pencil • faucet**

## DIRECTIONS

❶ Cut off the edge of the paper plate so you have a flat piece to work with. Draw a small circle on the center of the plate that is slightly larger than the diameter of the pencil.

❷ At the edge of the plate, make six evenly-spaced 1-inch-long cuts. Fold one side of each cut down, as shown.

❸ Cut out the hole in the center of the plate and slip the pencil halfway through. It should fit loosely in the hole.

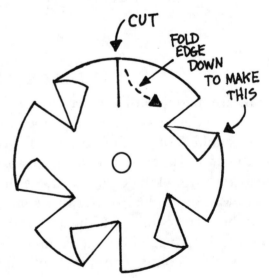

CUT

FOLD EDGE DOWN TO MAKE THIS

❹ Turn the water on to make a slow stream. Holding the pencil, ease the water wheel into the stream of water so it flows down over the folds in the paper.

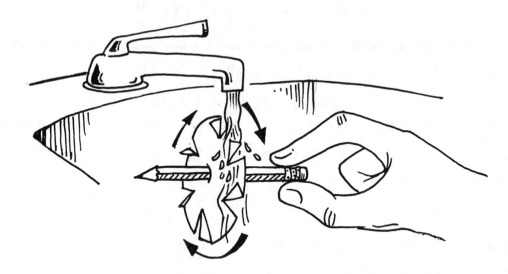

## WHAT'S GOING ON?

The flowing water pushes against the folds in the paper, making the wheel turn. The turning wheel can be used to do work. If there was a gear or a system of gears at the end of the pencil, that would have turned, too. (See Experiment 25, *Round and Round*.)

# PHANTOM
# COLORS

*Your eyes can play some strange tricks on you. Try this colorful experiment on your friends.*

## WHAT YOU'LL NEED

• **two sheets of 8½- by 11-inch white paper • ruler • three markers (yellow, green, and black)**

## DIRECTIONS

**❶** Perform this experiment in a very well-lit area. Place one sheet of paper on a flat surface. With the black marker, draw a square that is 4 inches on each side. Draw a 1-inch-wide border around that.

**❷** Color the square green and the border yellow.

**❸** Draw a small, solid black dot about the size of a pea in the center of the green square.

**❹** Hold up the paper and stare at the dot for about 1 minute. Try not to blink.

**❺** Put that piece of paper down, then hold up a blank sheet of paper in front of your eyes. Stare at the center of the paper and give your eyes a moment to focus. What do you see?

## WHAT'S GOING ON?

When you stare at the green-and-yellow square, then at the blank sheet of paper, you see a faint version of the square but in different colors. This time, the border is blue and the center square is red. Your eyes have special cells called rods and cones. Rods are the cells that go to work in low light, while the cones see color. When you stare at the black dot in the colored square, you make the cones in your eyes that see yellow and green work very hard. They get tired. When you stare at the blank piece of paper, your eyes still perceive the image, but the tired cones are resting. The cones that haven't been overused—the ones that see blue and red—go to work, and you see the "ghost" image in those colors.

# METAL IMAGE

*Have you ever seen yourself in a fun-house mirror? The silly image is an example of how the shape of a surface can affect the reflection of light.*

## WHAT YOU'LL NEED
**• hand mirror • clean, shiny tablespoon**

## DIRECTIONS

❶ Hold up the mirror and look at your image. How does it look?

❷ Now hold the tablespoon in front of you. Look at your image in the bowl of the spoon. Does your image look different than it did in the mirror?

❸ Turn the spoon around and look at your image on the back of the bowl. Now what do you see? How is your image different each time you look at it?

## WHAT'S GOING ON?

The image you see in the mirror is clear and accurate because the surface of the mirror is flat. It reflects, or bounces, the light rays straight back to your eye. Your eye sends these clear images to your brain to be interpreted. You perceive that image as a reflection of yourself in a mirror. The bowl of the spoon is not flat. The front of the spoon is concave, or curved inward. It bounces the light rays in different directions and your image appears distorted. The back of the spoon is convex, or curved outward. The light rays are reflected away from the center of your eye and your image appears upside down.

# F L U I D

# F L O W

*Can you move water from one bowl to another without pouring it out? You really can do it using air pressure.*

## WHAT YOU'LL NEED

• **two books (each at least 1 inch thick)** • **paper towels** • **two small bowls of the same size** • **pitcher** • **water** • **2 feet of ¼-inch-wide plastic tubing**

## DIRECTIONS

**1** Stack two books on a flat surface and cover them with a paper towel.

**2** Put one bowl on top of the paper towel. Use the pitcher to fill the bowl nearly to the rim with water.

**3** Place the second bowl on the flat surface about 1 foot from the first.

**4** Put one end of the tubing into the water-filled bowl. Put the other end of the tubing in your mouth and suck on it until you draw a tiny bit of water into your mouth. Don't swallow the water. Place your tongue over the opening of the tube to keep air from entering it. Open your mouth and slide your finger over the tube opening. Do this quickly so the water doesn't escape.

**❺** Place the end of the tube you are holding into the empty bowl and let go. Don't swallow any water that is in your mouth. Spit it into the bowl.

### WHAT'S GOING ON?

In this experiment, you create a siphon, a device that can move water from one area to another using air pressure. The water runs from the first bowl to the second without stopping. By sucking out the air in the tube, you lower the air pressure inside. The air pressure on the water in the bowl becomes higher than that in the tube and forces water into the tubing. Once you release the end of the tube, the force of gravity goes to work and the water easily runs out into the lower bowl.

# WHAT TIME
## IS IT?

**ADULT HELP REQUIRED**

*People have been telling time since long before the invention of clocks and watches. Here's a way for you and an adult helper to make your own "ancient" timepiece.*

## WHAT YOU'LL NEED

• **two 2-liter plastic soda bottles with caps** • **hammer** • **large nail**
• **fine playground sand** • **duct tape** • **timer** • **marker**

## DIRECTIONS

❶ Ask an adult to make a small hole in the top of each soda cap using the hammer and nail. The two holes should be exactly the same size, and they should be in the same spot on the caps.

❷ Fill the first bottle with sand to within 1 inch of the top. Leave the other bottle empty. Tightly screw the caps onto each bottle.

❸ Turn the empty bottle upside down and hold it over the sand-filled bottle. Be sure the holes in the caps line up exactly, then securely tape the bottles together with duct tape.

**4** Turn the bottles over so the bottle with sand is on top. It will probably be unstable at first, so ask your helper to hold it in place. Start the timer right away. Every 5 minutes, mark the level of sand on the side of the bottle that is filling with sand.

**5** When the bottle on top is completely empty, flip over the bottles so the unmarked bottle is on the bottom. Every 5 minutes, mark the level of sand on the side of the bottle that is filling with sand so both bottles are marked. You now have a timepiece.

## WHAT'S GOING ON?

With this simple timer, called a sand clock, the sand will always flow at the same rate. Since you mark each 5-minute interval on the bottles, you can use the sand clock to time different activities. The amount of time it takes for the entire bottle to empty depends on how much sand is in it and how large the holes are in the caps.

---

### Something Extra

Can you construct a timer using water instead of sand? Will water run through the holes in the caps at a different rate?

---

# MESSED-UP MUSIC

Ask an adult to give you a cassette tape that you can ruin. Try this demonstration to see why magnets and tapes don't mix.

## WHAT YOU'LL NEED

• cassette tape • cassette tape player • magnet

## DIRECTIONS

❶ Listen to the tape to be sure that you can hear the music clearly, then eject it.

❷ Run the magnet across the top, bottom, and sides of the cassette several times.

❸ Play the tape again. How does it sound? How is the music different from the first time you played it?

## WHAT'S GOING ON?

The second time you play the tape, the music is garbled or gone. This is because the tape is coated with an iron film. The iron film contains tiny iron "bits" that are arranged in a particular order so they can be read by the tape player. When you rub the magnet on the cassette, it attracts the iron particles, pulling them out of order and making them unreadable. This is how magnets damage cassette tapes, and that's why it's a good idea to keep magnets away from cassette tapes.

---

**Something Extra**

With an adult's permission, try this experiment with a computer disk or videotape. Does the same thing happen? Why or why not?

---

# IN THE EYE OF THE BEHOLDER

*An optical illusion is something that your brain thinks you are seeing based on the information it is receiving. But your brain can be tricked!*

## WHAT YOU'LL NEED

**• 3-inch-square piece of white posterboard • pencil • scissors
• photograph or picture cut out of a magazine**

## DIRECTIONS

❶ In the center of the posterboard, sketch a cross, as shown.

❷ Cut out the cross and throw it away.

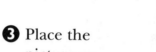

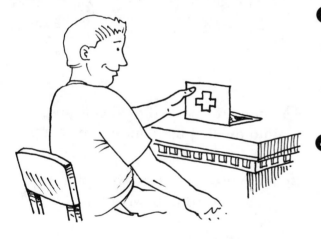

❸ Place the picture or photograph on a flat surface. Hold the posterboard frame in front of the picture at a right angle.

❹ Look down through the frame. The picture will appear to be three-dimensional (having height, width, and depth).

## WHAT'S GOING ON?

The brain receives information from the eyes. Your brain interprets, or figures out, what you see based on that information, but it can be tricked. You can usually tell that a picture is flat because you can see the edges. In this experiment, the posterboard frame hides the edges of the two-dimensional, or flat, picture. Without the edges as a guide, your brain may interpret what you are seeing as a view through a window of a real three-dimensional scene. As you stare at it, the photograph begins to look three-dimensional.

# CRAZY
# COLORS

*All the colors of the rainbow can be made by mixing just three primary colors in different combinations. Here's a way to make your own mix-and-match color kit.*

## WHAT YOU'LL NEED

• **three clear glass bowls (large enough to set the cups inside)** • **three clear plastic cups**
• **water** • **red, blue, and yellow food coloring**

## DIRECTIONS

❶ Fill each bowl and cup with water to about 2 inches below the top. On a flat surface, line up the three bowls in a row, with the three cups lined up in a row behind them.

❷ Put 5 drops of red food coloring into the first bowl and the first cup.

❸ Put 5 drops of blue food coloring into the second bowl and the second cup.

❹ Put 5 drops of yellow food coloring into the third bowl and the third cup.

❺ Once the food coloring has spread out evenly in each container, you are ready to test the color combinations. Start by lowering the cup filled with red water into the bowl filled with blue water. Don't let any water from the bowl spill over the rim of the cup, or vice versa.

**6** Look at the cup through the side of the bowl. What color do you see?

**7** Repeat Steps 5 and 6 using different color combinations.

## WHAT'S GOING ON?

When you mix primary colors (red, blue, and yellow), you see a combination of colors. When you combine red and blue, you create purple. This is the color you see in Step 5. When you combine red and yellow, you see orange. Blue and yellow create green when they are combined. All other colors can be created by mixing different amounts of these three colors.

### Something Extra

How many different colors can you make with your mix-and-match color kit? The kit contains three primary colors (red, blue, and yellow). The colors you make with different combinations of primary colors are called secondary colors.

# DRIP, DRIP, DRIP

*Honey, oil, and water are all fluids, but they pour out of a jar at very different rates. It's all because of viscosity.*

## WHAT YOU'LL NEED

• six 8-ounce paper cups • wire baker's rack • sharpened pencil • masking tape
• ½ cup water • ½ cup cooking oil • ½ cup honey

## DIRECTIONS

❶ Place three of the cups on a flat surface. Balance the baker's rack on top of them.

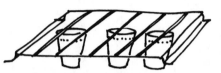

❷ Use the pencil to punch a hole into the bottom of each of the remaining cups. Cover the hole with masking tape on the outside of each cup.

❸ Place the second set of cups on top of the baker's rack, making a second row directly over the first row of cups. Line up the holes on the bottom of the cups so the fluids will empty into the cups below.

❹ Pour water into the first cup, cooking oil into the second cup, and honey into the third cup.

**5** Start with the cup of honey. Lift it slightly and pull the masking tape away from the hole. Do the same for the other two cups. Which cup empties first? Which cup empties last?

## WHAT'S GOING ON?

The cup with the water in it empties first, while the cup with the honey empties last. Fluids flow at different rates. Viscosity is the tendency of a fluid to resist flow. In this experiment, the water has the lowest viscosity (because it flows easily), while the honey has the highest viscosity (it resists flow and takes a long time to drip through the hole). The cup with the oil finishes between the other two.

---

### Something Extra

Do you think that heat might have an effect on the viscosity of a fluid? Do you think that slightly warming the honey might make it flow faster or more slowly? Try warming the honey in a microwave for 20 seconds, then do the experiment again.

---

# OFF
# TRACK

*Can you change an object's center of gravity? Check this out!*

## WHAT YOU'LL NEED
• **rubber ball** • **thumbtack**

## DIRECTIONS

❶ Roll the rubber ball across the floor and observe its path. Is it straight?

❷ Stick a thumbtack into the ball and roll it again. Does the path change?

## WHAT'S GOING ON?

When you roll the ball the first time, the center of gravity is at the center of the ball. With the thumbtack, you add a slight amount of weight to one side. This shifts the center of gravity and makes the ball roll in a different path. It rolls toward the side with the thumbtack.

---

### Something Extra

Add more thumbtacks to the ball to see how the path of the ball changes with each new tack.

---

# TWINKLE, TWINKLE, (58) LITTLE STAR

*The stars in the night sky are incredibly far from the Earth. How can scientists measure the distance to a star without actually going there? One of the tools they use to do this is parallax.*

## WHAT YOU'LL NEED
• soda bottle • shelf or table • quarter

## DIRECTIONS

**❶** Place the soda bottle on a shelf or table, then move at least 10 feet away from it. Hold the quarter out at arm's length.

**❷** Close your left eye. Line up the quarter so it blocks out at least part of the soda bottle from your view.

**❸** Close your right eye and open your left eye. Is the quarter still blocking the soda bottle from your view?

## WHAT'S GOING ON?

Although you don't move, the quarter no longer appears to block the soda bottle from view. This happens because you shift your point of view when you use your right eye instead of your left eye. This shift is called parallax. The closer you are to an object, the more it will appear to shift. As the Earth moves through its orbit during a year, astronomers can measure the position of a star from different points of view. Knowing how far the Earth has moved, and the apparent difference in the star's position, they can calculate the star's distance from the Earth.

# FOLLOW
............................................................................
## THAT STAR

*Early sailors used astrolabes to determine their location. Make one of your own and you will always have the stars to guide you. You may need a star-savvy adult's help.*

## WHAT YOU'LL NEED

**• string • plastic protractor (from a stationery store) • scissors • metal nut • pencil**

## DIRECTIONS

❶ Stretch the end of the string from the bottom of the flat side to the top of the rounded side of the protractor. Cut a piece of string that is double that length. Tie one end of the string to the nut. Loosely tie the other end of the string to the center of the flat side of the protractor.

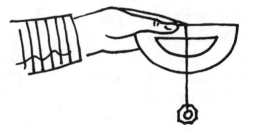

❷ Cut two small pieces of string and use them to tie the pencil to the flat, unnumbered side of the protractor.

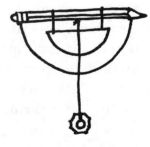

❸ On a clear night, hold the pencil up to your eyes and look along it to get a good line of sight. Point the tip of the pencil toward the North Star. If you don't know where it is, ask an adult to help you find the star. Holding the instrument in place, look at the side of it to get a reading. The string will be hanging in line with the number, or degree, of your latitude.

## WHAT'S GOING ON?

In this experiment, you create a simple form of an instrument called an astrolabe. Latitude is a series of imaginary lines running east and west around the Earth. People use these lines to figure out how far north or south they are from the equator. The protractor is used to measure angles. When you point the pencil at the North Star, the string measures the angle between the North Star and the horizon.

# 60 P U F F E D
# U P

*Plants need water to help them grow. Do seeds need water, too? This experiment will give you some insight into the nature of seeds.*

## WHAT YOU'LL NEED
• spice bottle or any small container with a plastic snap-on cap
• dried beans (small enough to fit into the bottle, such as red beans) • water

## DIRECTIONS

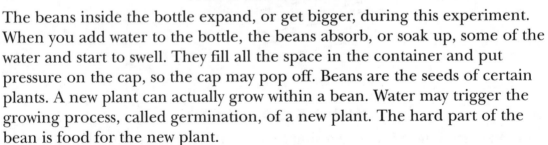

❶ Fill up the bottle or container to the rim with dried beans.

❷ Fill up the container to the rim with water and snap on the cap.

❸ Don't disturb the container for at least 8 hours.

## WHAT'S GOING ON?

The beans inside the bottle expand, or get bigger, during this experiment. When you add water to the bottle, the beans absorb, or soak up, some of the water and start to swell. They fill all the space in the container and put pressure on the cap, so the cap may pop off. Beans are the seeds of certain plants. A new plant can actually grow within a bean. Water may trigger the growing process, called germination, of a new plant. The hard part of the bean is food for the new plant.

---

### Something Extra

To watch the process of germination, line a drinking glass with blotting paper and stuff the inside of the glass with cotton wool. Slip a bean between the blotting paper and the glass, about 2 inches down from the rim. Add water until the level is about ½ inch below the seed. Be sure that the cotton wool and blotting paper are moist. Place the glass in a warm spot out of direct sunlight. Keep the blotting paper moist and observe the seed over one or two weeks. What happens?

---